T0137726

Books by Jean Bacon White
A Bible Series

All the hope in the Bible
Ordinary people doing extraordinary things

Meet the trinity
God the father, God the son, God the Holy Spirit

What is wisdom?
Where are the wise?

What is Wisdom

Where Are the Wise?

JEAN BACON WHITE

WESTBOW
PRESS®
A DIVISION OF THOMAS NELSON
& ZONDERVAN

Copyright © 2017 Jean Bacon White.

All rights reserved. No part of this book may be used or reproduced by any means, graphic, electronic, or mechanical, including photocopying, recording, taping or by any information storage retrieval system without the written permission of the author except in the case of brief quotations embodied in critical articles and reviews.

This book is a work of non-fiction. Unless otherwise noted, the author and the publisher make no explicit guarantees as to the accuracy of the information contained in this book and in some cases, names of people and places have been altered to protect their privacy.

Unless otherwise noted scripture quotations are taken from the Holy Bible, New International Version. NIV. Copyright 1973, 1978, 1984 by International Bible Society. Used by permission of Zondervan. All rights reserved.

Scripture taken from the King James Version of the Bible

WestBow Press books may be ordered through booksellers or by contacting:

WestBow Press
A Division of Thomas Nelson & Zondervan
1663 Liberty Drive
Bloomington, IN 47403
www.westbowpress.com
1 (866) 928-1240

Because of the dynamic nature of the Internet, any web addresses or links contained in this book may have changed since publication and may no longer be valid. The views expressed in this work are solely those of the author and do not necessarily reflect the views of the publisher, and the publisher hereby disclaims any responsibility for them.

Any people depicted in stock imagery provided by Thinkstock are models, and such images are being used for illustrative purposes only.
Certain stock imagery © Thinkstock.

ISBN: 978-1-5127-8203-5 (sc)
ISBN: 978-1-5127-8204-2 (e)

Print information available on the last page.

WestBow Press rev. date: 04/05/2017

Dedication

To my dear brother, Dick, my most dedicated fan and encourager.

Contents

INTRODUCTION

As we study the mind and its important station in our inner self, we find more and more mysteries. We have the mind, the self, the spirit, and the soul, which are also invisible and entangled with one another in ways that mold us into who we are as human beings; the self, perceiving, knowledge, understanding, discerning, interest, comprehending, thinking and sense are also part of the maze which is active 24/7 in our brains.

We see ourselves as intelligent, caring, and normal individuals until something in the mix no longer jibes with the rest. Dementia, downs syndrome, dyslexia, autism, and many diseases can also affect the normal coordination of all these forces within us; love, hate, temper, serenity, anger, reason, conscience, fear, faith etcetera. We could go on and on to try to cover all that the mind holds; both good and bad. We have to learn to have common sense and understand what is nonsense, trust those that are really friends and mistrust those with their own agenda. Learning is the basis for knowing and knowing and understanding lead to wisdom. Our priority for this book is the search for wisdom, the easiest way to find it is to first realize that there are two kinds of wisdom; worldly wisdom and spiritual wisdom. Through this search, we will discover how the rest fits into these two categories and take a journey to find where are the wise.

PREFACE

The brain is a material part of the body contained within the skull. It is sensitized to absorb all information sent to it from inside and outside of the body. It contains the means to process this information and pass it on to the mind, which is not a material part of the body, but lies somewhere in the brain. You can lose it, abuse it or use it in your search for wisdom.

If you lose it, we may find that you are demented, diseased, or even insane or a fool who has destroyed it with things that have taken away its usefulness. Men have been studying these mysteries for centuries.

No one has been able to unlock the matter of the brain, the shadow of the mind, or the secrets therein, where we also have a soul and a conscience.

The brain is a receiver, the mind is the decision maker, the conscience passes judgement. There is also a spirit that is the self, which is in control, and in the Christian, a Holy Spirit which guards the soul.

Much has been written about the brain in the physical. Scientific, and psychological realms, concerning what the so- called grey matter in our heads is all about. This book is not concerned with those things, only the parts that no one can figure out.

CHAPTER 1

The Mind

Sonny is ten years old. He smells the cookies in the kitchen. His mind decides they are his favorite chocolate chip and he must have one. His spirit says he deserves it. He knows that mom will say he needs to wait, for it is almost supper time. He sneaks one anyway when she isn't looking, and she catches him. He says, "Aw mom, I'm hungry." He could have put it behind him and declared his innocence, but his conscience does not tell him that he is naughty, because he is hungry.

When he is fifteen, he sneaks money from her purse. He knows this is wrong and there will be consequences if he is caught, but he does it anyway. Now his conscience will remind him that he is guilty and he will be fearful that he will be found out.

The mind is our instrument of learning to be wise. Criminals learn to cover their tracks so they will not get caught, but most of them do get caught eventually and have to pay the penalty for their crimes. Our prisons are full and new ones are being built all the time.

There are some people who have no conscience to keep them from evil behavior. Arrogance, selfishness and greed separate them from the norm. They can be filthy rich or just plain filthy in their lifestyle, or they may seem to be what they are not. They may fool people into thinking they are trustworthy. They lie, cheat and steal and innocent people suffer by trusting them. They have worldly wisdom to keep one step ahead of the law until the day their sin finds them out.

We have a population which we call street people. Among them are the homeless the helpless and the hopeless. Many of them are there through no fault of their own. They need to be street wise to survive and Some of them do not. Society has not yet found a solution to the problems it must face on every level: social, medical, political, religious, financial, and bureaucratic, but especially wise decisions that show common sense and compassion. Where are the wise?

The breakdown of the family has contributed to most of the troubles we find ourselves in. This is where we were meant to live and move and learn about love, life and contentment. The society reflects the state of the home. Family values used to be reflected in the community. Whoever said, "It takes a village to raise a child," got it right. A generation ago moms and dads were of the same mind and had the same rules for their children as their neighbors. Children learned to respect their parents and adults in general. Teachers were involved with their families and if punishment was needed both home and school participated. Boys learned to treat girls gently and to play fair. They all learned manners and that bad words were not acceptable and laws were not made to be broken.

Being wise in the ways of the world is called survival. Spiritual wisdom is knowing God's promises and purpose for life. There are many who are lost and lonely with something missing in their lives. Drug companies make millions with their potions to bring peace of mind; relief from stress and anxiety.

The Bible offers peace free of charge. Spiritual wisdom is the answer. All it takes is a change of mind.

Pr.23:7 As a man thinks in his heart, so is he.

Rom.12:2 Be transformed by the renewing of your mind.

The heart of man in spiritual terms is that place in the mind that is central to his being, just as the physical heart is essential to his physical life. The mind wonders and wanders, searching for answers to life's tough questions: who, what, where, when, how, and why am I?

When we are young, we want to be grown up, so we can have more freedom. But, freedom requires responsibility. That is why growing up is one of the hardest things we might ever have to do. Age in numbers has little meaning as we learn in so many different ways. The mind is influenced by everything we see, hear, learn, and experience in our home and in the world. We walk and talk and use our head and hands and grow into adolescence, where we find changes taking place in our bodies and our minds.

We are caught in a place between childhood and adulthood and changing expectations from inside ourselves and from others. Our mind is overtaken by questions and emotions about who we are, where we belong and what we will be when we grow up.

The report card becomes a measure of our intelligence and how much progress is being made in comparison to others. Our circle of friends becomes those who seem equal to us. We need to fit in with our peers and please our teachers and our parents. So many things are changing so fast that many become overwhelmed and drop out of school and give up the process and become cases of arrested development, hanging around home and living off mom and dad. Others turn to drugs or take to the streets, joining gangs or just disappearing. The search for wisdom goes on.

Scripture from NIV

CHAPTER 2

The Self

I am an essential person distinct from others. I am myself. When I look in a mirror, what I see is me, myself. What makes me different from all the other people in the world depends on what is going on in my head. I could be a twin and look exactly like my sibling but we are not exactly alike. I may have the same habits or character as many other people; the color of my eyes skin and hair etcetera. I may be the same size, height, sex or have the same occupation or education as hundreds or even thousands of people. But there are no two persons on the planet exactly alike. All the things that happen in the brain, in my skull are unique, even though the gray matter may be made of the same material.

What happens in the brain is influenced by genetics, environment, diet, culture, family, knowledge and experience and much more. We may be self-conscious in situations that are new or different than what we are used to. How we adapt to change depends on many things; age, upbringing, level of understanding, knowledge and self- confidence. There are cases of children who have been hidden away for years and have passed what should have been the stages of mental development, unable to cope with all they have missed, and many never are able to adjust to what we call normal. It all goes back to the concept that a child must receive love and caring in order to develop the way they are supposed to.

Years ago, doctors believed a child developed the self by age 3, but more recently discovered that if they have not received love and nurturing by the age of six months, their development is already impaired. Of course, head injuries and trauma also can cause damage that cannot be fixed. And we are constantly being reminded of what certain addictions do to the mind.

Learning begins at birth; our mind is a clean slate. All we know how to do is to take nourishment and cry to have our needs met. Nurturing and love mold us and lack of it hurts us. If we are not taught to share with others, we become selfish. If we do not learn to deal with failure, we might never learn to be able to function normally. When we get it wrong, we have to learn to get it right. Self-control, self-indulgence, self-confidence and self- discipline are all learned behaviors. Bad habits, bad attitudes, arrogance, love and hate are also involved in learning to be able to find our way in this world.

Psychiatrists can give us descriptions of all kinds of self- problems that mess up people's lives. What happens in the mind is what triggers emotions and the emotions that prevail affect everything else in the self; self- indulgence, self-worth, self-condemnation, self-love, self- hate and self-seeking. The age of fifteen is crucial. It is the time to know who you are and how you handle the transition from child to adult. It is a rocky road that requires much care to reinforce the good stuff in them and in their lives, because they will never be more vulnerable. They need to know who to trust and that their heart has a home; that their mistakes can be forgiven and their talents appreciated. The organizations of Big Brothers and Big Sisters have done a great job of filling the void in many families. There are special places for children to find help when they can no longer stay with family. The courts remove them from dangerous environments and work to find the right place for meeting their specific needs. Environment plays a large part in the development of the self.

We can't leave out the part that genetics plays as well. We hear parents say, "You are just like your father" or, "You are just like your mother" and some of this is because of similar temperament and some of it comes from example. Parents or other caregivers play a distinct role in the development of the self. The everyday life in the home is the first influence in the life of a child. There they learn feelings of self-worth and self-confidence or the opposite. Some homes are not pleasant places because of poor parenting and neglect and even abuse. Some children find good mentors in grand-parents, neighbors, teachers or friends. There are many who rise above poor beginnings.

Troubled souls find rest and compassion when the people of God come into their lives. They learn that we have a God of second chances that can turn a life around and replace the bad stuff with good stuff, because God loves everyone he has created and saying yes to him and no to the world that makes you sad, can bring you into a life that makes you glad.

Rom. 6:6 For we know that our old self was crucified with him so that the body of sin might be done away with, that we should no longer be slaves to sin, because anyone who dies has been freed from sin.

Eph. 4:22-24 You were taught with regard to your former life to put off your old deceitful desires, to be made new in the attitude of your minds and to put on the new self, created to be like God in true righteousness and holiness.

Col. 3:9-10 Do not lie to each other, since you have taken off your old self with its practices, and have put on the new self which is being renewed in knowledge, in the image of its creator.

Life is a journey we must all face and whether we have made mistakes along the way or have suffered because of others, Jesus came to teach us that we are loved by our creator and he waits for us to ask him to come into our lives and help us to be all that we can be. There is help for every problem and someone out there that can show you the way. It makes no difference what your circumstances have been or what they are now, Jesus in your life can make all things new.

Scripture from NIV

CHAPTER 3

Knowledge

How do I know that I really know what I think I know? We go to school to learn what we need to know to survive in the world we live in. Our world consists of our family, friends, our environment, those who have charge of our living and learning, and the culture we are brought up in. We have to learn a language and what is expected of us by those we have personal contact with, and the society around us.

This is a matter of survival. We must know where to go, what to do, what to say and how to behave. We must get along with our peers and those who are in authority, for our life depends on it. But knowing is not enough. We must learn to do something with what we know in order to make a life.

As a child, we must know who we are and where we live, in case we get lost. As we get older we learn how to follow directions so we don't get lost. When we are elderly there are GPS systems if we drive and cell phones we can carry so people can find us anywhere if we lose our way.

Changes are always taking place that cause us to need more knowledge and we are never too old to learn more. Knowledge is necessary to make a living and make a life, to find peace of mind and make good choices and decisions.

Worldly knowledge is gained by study and experience and we can all be wise about some things. We figure out what pleases the people around us and what behaviors are acceptable and those that are not, especially when they have consequences. We learn to understand the differences between the right way and the wrong way to do things and laws and rules that need to be obeyed, or else. All through life there is somebody in charge of everything, whether we like it or not: there is a boss at home, at school, on the street, and on the job. Even the boss has a boss somewhere in most cases. If you are the boss, you have to know how to earn respect and cooperation in order to be a success.

Knowing the ways of the world and how to get by is not enough to satisfy the soul; that special place within the caverns of the mind where joy and peace are satisfied. According to Webster, the soul is the essence of life. According to scripture the soul is the seat of reason and will.

It has been said many times that, "A little knowledge is a dangerous thing." Knowledge alone can be dangerous. Too much knowledge can also be a danger to the soul. Picture the man who gave his whole life to learning. He got all the college degrees possible and spent most of his time in books and libraries. He finally ended up on a quiz show and made a lot of money. When the quiz master asked, what he would do with the money, his answer was, "Buy more books." He did not have a life beyond gathering knowledge. He died a lonely old man in a house full of books. He could have become a teacher, a mentor, anything that might have used his knowledge for some good to others as well as himself. He was like the miser who starved to death while hiding all his money in his mattress. Neither of them ever satisfied his soul. Wisdom was missing in their lives.

There is nothing wrong with loving to learn. Many have learned to do wonderful things, because they did something with the knowledge they had gained: cures for diseases, building better, living better, eating better, taking better care of ourselves and what we own, and who we are, inventions, medicines, and so much more.

We appreciate progress and intelligence that helps people and nations, but people and nations also need wisdom to bring peace, joy, and understanding to our world.

Knowledge also needs understanding. We can memorize the dictionary and encyclopedias and still not understand what they have to do with us. We, ourselves need both knowledge and understanding before we can even consider wisdom.

Doing what is right and just and fair is a step in the right direction.

Gen. 2:17…but you must not eat from it, (the tree of the knowledge of good and evil) for when you eat of it you will surely die.

Ex. 31:2-3 See, I have chosen Bezalel, son of Uri, the son of Hur, of the tribe of Judah, and I have filled him with the spirit of God, with skill, ability and knowledge in all kinds of crafts. (God said to Moses)

God gives gifts to all of us. Adam and eve had the tree of life and could have lived in that beautiful garden forever, in peace and love, if they had made the right choice, which was obedience to God instead of the beautiful creature in the tree.

Moses was a great leader as long as he followed God's plan for his people. He made a wrong choice and lost sight of God's plan when he got angry and obeyed his emotions. He did not speak to the rock, but in his anger, he struck it with the staff and plenty of water poured out. But God was not given the credit for being there for his people. Because of his disobedience, Moses lost his right to go into the promised land.

The Bible teaches us that there is good and evil and we must use our knowledge to make good choices, because there is no peace when we choose the wrong instead of the right. Knowledge is good, but without wisdom we would be doomed. We need to know what to do with what we know.

2 Chr. 1:10-12 Solomon asked God, "Give me wisdom and knowledge that I may lead these people, for who is able to govern this great people of yours?"

God gave it to him and also made him the wisest and richest king in the world, because of his obedience. But when he was old he made alliances with other nations. And by marrying the king's daughters until he had a thousand wives and concubines, he used up his fortune building palaces for them and temples for their gods. He would have been wise to trust God for peace in his kingdom.

Pr. 1:2-6 The prologue to the Proverbs states, ...for attaining wisdom and discipline; for understanding; words of insight; for a disciplined and prudent life doing what is just and right and fair; for giving prudence to the simple, knowledge and discretion to the young. let the wise listen and add to their learning and let the discerning get guidance for understanding proverbs and parables, the sayings and riddles of the wise.

Prov.1:2-7 Knowledge and understanding need each other on the way to wisdom.

CHAPTER 4

Understanding

Understanding is a step up from knowledge. We know that the light goes on when we flick the switch and it is electricity that the power comes from. But we also must understand, that if there is a problem more serious than a burned out light bulb which we know how to change, we had better get an electrician to mess with it, because we also know that people get electrocuted by touching live wires. We may not understand about transformers and power plants, but we leave those things to the experts. We understand the danger involved in making those things work correctly.

We learn early not to cross the street when the light is green. That means vehicles only, yellow means caution and red means we stop and they can go. Our lives depend on knowing and obeying.

We learn to read and write, but we need to understand what the words mean to make sense of it. Our mind is the seat of learning and we must use it in every facet of our lives. Sometimes it is embarrassing to have to ask questions, but that is how we learn a lot of things. The toddler is always asking "why?" He wants to know! It is far better to ask someone about something we know nothing about than to get it wrong. Asking questions is an important part of learning.

Understanding means intelligence, ability, to comprehend and to judge.

Job 32:8 But it is the spirit in a man, the breath of the almighty, that gives him understanding.

Ps. 49:20 A man who has riches without understanding is like the beasts that perish.

i19:130 The unfolding of your words gives light. It gives understanding to the simple. .

Isa. 29:24 Those who are wayward in spirit will gain understanding. Those who complain will accept instruction.

Jer. 3:15 Then I will give you shepherds after my own heart who will lead you with knowledge and understanding.

Dan. 5:12 This man Daniel, whom the king called Belteshazzar was found to have a keen mind and knowledge and understanding.

Phi. 4:7 And the peace of God which transcends all understanding, will guard your hearts and your minds in Christ Jesus.

Phi. 1:6 I pray that you may be active in showing your faith, so that you will have a full understanding of every good thing we have in Christ.

Perception is a part of understanding. Some hold to this, "Seeing is believing," But can you always believe what you are seeing? Hallucinations and illusions are not what they seem. There are mirages in the desert, shadows at twilight and your boyfriend or girlfriend kissing someone who turns out to be a relative. When you really understand, what you see, you have good perception.

If you attend a trial at the courthouse and are called as a witness, you must be sure of what you saw, for many other witnesses may not have perceived it in the same way. We must always be sure that we understand what is going on around us for safety and for peace of mind. Perception is being aware and realizing the reality of something that you see with your eyes, and also what you read. You need to know the difference between fiction and fact. You may read a book that seems like it is real, but is really a story that someone made up.

This also concerns the mind. When you are having a conversation, sometimes people say, "I see," when they don't really understand what we are talking about. Perceiving is also understanding with the mind, figuring things out whether the eyes are involved or not.

You see that something is not right in a situation, by the tension in the room. You see that something good is happening when the mood changes for the better. You see that something is wrong when the children in the other room are too quiet. You perceive danger when you hear a gunshot. Perception can use all the senses.

When we have trouble, understanding something, we need to get help, so we do. Getting another opinion could help in learning something new or bring more clarity to something old. The more we learn, the more confidence we have in our opinions and our perception.

For years, they called Pluto a planet and now they do not, because they finally realized that what they were seeing did not fit their perception of what a planet is. A wood carver or a sculptor can see something in their material and then bring it out for all to see.

A scientist strives to find a cure for disease and works sometimes for years before he finds it. These people have a perception that is exceptional, because they see what nobody else can and bring it to us.

We are wise enough to figure out the difference between reality and wishful thinking and become wise to our own limitations, our weaknesses and our strong points and make a life.

Job 33:14-15 For God does speak-now one way, now another-though man may not perceive it. In a dream, in a vision of the night, when deep sleep falls on men as they slumber in their beds.

Discerning is also a part of understanding. It is discovering with the eye or the mind. The wise have a discerning heart and mind.

Prov.10:13 Wisdom is found on the lips of the discerning.

14:6 Knowledge comes easily to the discerning.

15:14 The discerning heart seeks knowledge.

17:28 The discerning will hold his tongue.

19:25 Rebuke a discerning man and he will gain knowledge.

28:7 He who keeps the law is discerning.

CHAPTER 5

Folly

Folly is the opposite of wisdom. It is the behavior of fools. Impetuous people act without thinking and make foolish choices, because they do not think about consequences until it is too late. The wise think before they act and have better results. The fool has no plan, but acts spontaneously on his emotions. If it feels good do it. That kind of mind set brings troubles, addictions, enemies, jail and even diseases and death. The boy who climbed the light pole on a dare made a foolish mistake and was electrocuted. The teen who drank too much at the party ended up pregnant. The man who thought he would not get addicted if he just tried out the new drug is now in an institution for the insane. More than one friend has aids.

We can have fun and be funny and even be good at the same time. Fools make dirty jokes and become rude and insulting to innocent people. Other fools laugh at them. There are also good comedians that the whole family can enjoy. There are good jokes as well as bad jokes. We must be careful of what goes into our minds, because it affects what comes out.

In the Bible, sin is called folly, because it does no good and produces evil. It is sin that destroys the inner peace which we all seek and destroys relationships with others and with our Lord. Pleasure may last for a season but in the end your sin will find you out and the payment comes due.

The prologue to Proverbs, which is a book about wisdom, explains it well:

Pr. 1:1-6 The proverbs of Solomon son of David, king of Israel, for attaining wisdom and discipline; for understanding words of insight; for acquiring a disciplined and prudent life, doing what is right and just and fair; for giving prudence to the simple, knowledge and discretion to the young. Let the wise listen and add to their learning, and let the discerning get guidance for understanding proverbs and parables, the sayings and riddles of the wise.

The fear of the Lord is the beginning of knowledge. The opposite of the wise man is the fool.

The husband has refused to give food and water to David and his men, out of his abundance. His wife Abigail secretly pleads for his life saying that folly goes with her husband and she will see to it that he gets the supplies that he needs, and David accepts her offer. The wisdom in that home belongs to her. (1 Sam 25:25)

Fools and folly go together and range from being foolish or absurd to even lacking common sense. Solomon wrote the book of Proverbs especially for the young to find wisdom and the wise to become wiser. In his old age, he realized his own folly.

Job's friend has decided that all the bad things that have happened to him must be punishment for sin. God calls the man a fool and tells him that his servant Job will pray and make sacrifice for him. (Job 42:8)

Ps. 85:18 The fool will die for lack of discipline and pay for his folly!

Isa.32:6 For the fool speaks folly. His mind is busy with evil: he practices ungodliness and spreads error concerning the Lord: the hungry he leaves empty and from the thirsty he withholds water.

Eccl. 2:12-14 Solomon says, "Then I turned my thoughts to consider wisdom, and also madness and folly. What more can the king's successor do than what has already been done? I saw that wisdom was better than folly, just as light is better than darkness. The wise man has eyes in his head, while the fool walks in darkness, but I found that the same fate overtakes them both.

7:25 So I turned my mind to understand wisdom, to investigate and search out wisdom and the scheme of things and to understand the stupidity of wickedness and the madness of folly.

12:13-14 Now all has been heard; here is the conclusion of the matter. Fear God and keep his commandments, for this is the whole duty of man. For God, will bring every deed to judgment, including every hidden thing, whether it is good or evil.

Ps. 14:1 The fool says in his heart, "There is no God." They are corrupt, their deeds revile. There is no one who does good.

The fear of the lord is the beginning of knowledge but fools despise wisdom and discipline.

Pr. 1:32 The waywardness of the simple will kill them and the complacency of fools will destroy.

Pr. 3:35 The wise inherit honor but fools he holds up to shame.

10:8 the wise in heart accepts commands but a chattering fool comes to ruin.

Pr. 10:23 A fool finds pleasure in evil conduct, but a man of understanding delights in wisdom.

12:15-16 The way of a fool seems right to him, but a wise man listens to advice. A fool shows his annoyance at once, but a prudent man overlooks an insult.

18:2 A fool finds no pleasure in understanding, but delights in airing his own opinion. Ezek. 13:3 This is what the sovereign Lord says, "Woe to the foolish prophets who follow their own spirit and have seen nothing."

Mat. 7:26 But everyone who hears these words of mine and does not put them into practice is like a foolish man who built his house upon the sand.

1 Pet. 2:15 For it is God's will that by doing good you should silence the ignorant talk of foolish men.

CHAPTER 6

Wisdom

There are many spirits in the Bible. The Holy Spirit is supreme because it is the spirit of God in the trinity. It is also called the spirit of truth several times. There are good spirits sent by God and demonic spirits from his enemy.

The human spirit is vulnerable, without the power of the Holy Spirit, and its condition becomes whatever human emotions are allowed to follow: broken. Lying, crushed, lowly, in despair, arrogant. It happens, that people in the same family can be so different when they grow up in the same home, with the same parents, under the same terrible conditions, and some children are able to rise above the poor parenting while others run wild with no direction. Some children, because wisdom comes by way of someone or some event that happens to touch their hearts, with a longing to know something better, seek knowledge and understanding which leads to wisdom. In God's economy, there is no such thing as a hopeless case. When someone chooses to follow the Lord, he is on the path to wisdom and righteousness.

God's enemy is watchful for our weaknesses and uses his powers of persuasion to turn us away from God. If we are weak in our faith, he can move us in a direction away from the one the Lord has for us. If we are weak in our beliefs, he can tempt us to sin. Some people crave the things of this world instead of wisdom and forfeit the blessings that come with an obedient heart.

We can learn from our mistakes and turn to God for forgiveness and become wise from lessons learned by foolish choices and bad behavior. A heart turned to the Lord can find blessings where curses were before. We can find wisdom when trouble comes. Holy Spirit power can change lives.

When we think, we can take care of everything ourselves, we prolong the problem that Jesus can take care of and bring peace where there is no peace and joy where there has been none before. The Bible is full of stories of people who learned to trust the Lord and found life worth living in all kinds of circumstances, because with him, we are never alone.

True believers are the family of God and the love and caring that comes from them is what the Lord has given us to share with others. We can recognize them, because they give of themselves and ask nothing in return. They are everywhere helping people in need, even in dangerous situations no matter what is going on around them. They are true friends. They show up when bad things happen: fires, floods tornadoes, earthquakes, avalanches, mudslides, blizzards, poverty, plagues, homelessness, epidemics, deaths, destruction, wars and more. They build churches and meeting houses, shelters, food pantries, soup kitchens and give jobs to the disabled and never give up spreading the love of God and his wisdom on the battle field and the mission field all over the word. The colleges and universities in our country were first founded to train Christians to share their faith and bring spiritual wisdom to the young.

The word wisdom appears two hundred and twenty times in the Bible and wise appears one hundred and ninety- eight times, so they must be very important to the Lord.

Chapter 7

Righteousness

Spiritual wisdom comes from the righteousness of God through the sacrifice of his son on the cross. Salvation comes before spiritual wisdom can occur for spiritual wisdom comes from that Holy Spirit that lives in the heart of the believer.

In the Old Testament, God's righteousness and justice are shown by his will and his way. It is an absolute necessity for the perfect couple in the perfect garden at the beginning of Genesis to listen and learn his will and his way in order to keep the perfect life they have been given. God walks with them like a father guiding his children and teaches them how to keep the joy that they have. He has them name the animals who are friendly and they are not to fear. Everything they need is there for them to partake of except the tree of the knowledge of good and evil. If evil enters the garden, they will forfeit not only their perfect life, but life itself, for evil means death. God's righteousness is perfection and he is never wrong. His promises are sure.

God's righteousness prevails forever and man has none of his own. It only comes as a gift for the obedient. He may show his wrath at times and disobedience brings sorrow. But his perfection is just and forgiveness can restore the humble, who repent of their errors.

When the flood came in Noah's time, because he was a preacher of righteousness, who obeyed God, he was saved with his family to repopulate the world once again. He saved the animals in the ark while the world was cleansed with water. Noah was a righteous man. (Gen 6 KJV)

Abraham, Isaac and Jacob went through hard times while learning that it is always best when we do things God's way. Kings chose their own way instead of God's way and their kingdoms crumbled. Prophets and priests brought God's commands to their minds and if they repented and were obedient to God, they were blessed and when they did not they had to take the consequences. Without righteousness, they were doomed to failure. (Gen 15-35 KJV)

The prophets: Nehemiah, Isaiah, Jeremiah, Ezekiel, Daniel. Hosea, Joel, Amos, Obadiah, Jonah, Micah, Nahum, Habakkuk, Zephaniah, Haggai, Zechariah, and Malachi were the prophets who learned God's righteousness and taught it to others and they each have books named after them in the Bible.

CHAPTER 8

Jesus the righteousness of God

Matthew presents Jesus as king over all. He represents God's righteousness in the flesh. No other man would ever be perfect. He announced that he had to be about his father's business when he was twelve years old, when he stayed to speak to the teachers in Jerusalem and missed his ride home until his family came back to find him. He obeyed his parents and began his public ministry, when he was thirty three years old.

His life reflected the words of the old testament prophets perfectly so that all the wise would know that the Messiah had come.

He healed the sick and even raised the dead. He preached from a boat and even walked on water. He preached in homes and outside on mountains and in fields and by the waters.

He moved about from town to town and gathered the twelve who became his constant companions and crowds followed him. He turned one lunch into three thousand and again for five thousand.

He healed the blind, the lame and even leprosy which was a plague on the population, the most hideous, disease in their world.

He fulfilled the law of Moses. He saved the souls of those who believed and promised that the Holy spirit of God would come upon them. The story of Pentecost shows how it happened. He appointed twelve faithful followers to become evangelists and preach his gospel all over the world. Peter, James, John, Thomas, Matthew, Mark, Luke, Judas, Andrew, Philip, Bartholomew, Simon the zealot, Jude, and James the less were chosen as his inner circle.

Mark sees the Lord as a servant. Jesus came not to condemn the world, but so the world could be saved from the wages of sin, which means death either physically or spiritually or both. He begins his ministry in Galilee. He is baptized by John the Baptist, who is his cousin and has been chosen by God to be the forerunner who taught of his coming. God had described what would happen at this baptism in order for John to know that this was truly his son. The Holy spirit came down as a dove and lit upon him and God spoke saying, "This is my beloved son in whom I am well pleased." God's righteousness passed on to his son.

The devil realizes that this could mess up his kingdom of darkness that he is building in the world and tries to tempt him to join with him and share his power. But the perfect man has the fullness of the righteousness of God in him and refuses to be fooled by this pretender.

With the twelve chosen for his ministry he begins by performing a miracle, by turning water into wine at a wedding.

He preaches in parables to clarify his gospel and more miracles occur and Herod trembles thinking John the Baptist has come back from the dead after he had him beheaded. By this time, Jesus had fed the five thousand and walked on water.

He travels about ministering to individuals and the crowds that follow him. Many are healed and he even drives out evil spirits. He even blesses little children as they come to him.

Finally, he goes to Jerusalem where he knows the end will come and he will be captured and hung on a cross and die for us, after giving us God's message that frees mankind to receive the righteousness and justice of the father. This is the perfection that God wants us to follow. Salvation is the beginning of our search for spiritual wisdom.

Luke sees him as a man of God. This God man is our example and our way of salvation. Luke gives us an account of his birth according to prophecy; his growing up as the carpenter Joseph's son and his relationship to his mother and siblings. He tells of the discovery of his mission. He gives the details of his ministry in various places that Mark mentioned briefly; the way he was received, his teachings, more parables and healings.

He tells us that John the Baptist is born and grows up to be the forerunner, who announces to the world that the Messiah has been born, and chronicles his path to the end; the controversies with the Jews, the last supper, Judas betrayal, his trial, his crucifixion, his rising from the dead, a new ministry with witnesses, and his ascension.

John the apostle, in his book sees Jesus as God. 1:1-2 (KJV) In the beginning was the word and the word was God. The same was in the beginning with God.

John is a man so righteous that he ministered to the ministers of the gospel. He was a cousin to Jesus and his family lived in Jerusalem where they had a fish market and he fished with his father and his brother James, another righteous man who was the first of the twelve to die for his faith.

John was with Jesus from the beginning of his ministry through the crucifixion and was the only one of the twelve to be there with the women. He lived to be in his eighties and died of natural causes. Many pastors tell new converts to read his gospel. He was the closest friend Jesus had and witnessed everything that happened to him. His book is sometimes referred to as the constitution of Christianity.

Wisdom cannot come before righteousness for we must be right with God through Christ because as Isaiah said in chapter 64, our righteousness is like filthy rags. We must be purified by the blood of his sacrifice and have salvation before we can have access to the righteousness of God in him. It cannot be earned. It comes by faith and surrender to the will of the Lord, who already has a plan for every life.

Paul comes as author of the letters to churches in the New Testament. He met Jesus on the road to Damascus in a vision that changed his life's mission from chasing Christians to becoming a servant of the Lord and with his righteousness founded churches everywhere he went. He ended up being beheaded by the Romans, giving his all for his savior.

CHAPTER 9

Grace

Grace is free and unmerited favor, reconciliation with the creator, who loves us in spite of ourselves. God's grace breaks down the barrier that sin has built between God and man. The event of the crucifixion pulled down those walls that separated us. God is holy and righteous and sin is not acceptable. It pleases God's enemy and leads people away from God. Grace is the compassion God has for his creation, regardless of who we are or the state of our being.

Grace protects forever the saved ones in the sight of God, because of their position in Christ. Ro. 6:14 (KJV) For sin shall not have dominion over you; for ye are not under law, bit under grace.

5:18 (KJV) Therefore as by offense of one judgment (the law) came upon all men to condemnation, even so, by righteousness of one (Jesus) the free gift came upon all men unto justification of life.

Mat. 5:48 (KJV) Be ye therefore perfect as your father which is in heaven is perfect.

The law of Moses was a system that showed that we were sinners and could never be obedient to all the commandments all the time, because we live in a body of flesh and the flesh without the Holy Spirit is weak and with it our strength is made perfect in his righteousness. We needed a savior to pay for our sins and show us what a perfect man looks like. There is no way we ca n be perfect in the eyes of the God without Jesus. He is our advocate with the father and because he himself is God in person, he can stand us before him so that the father sees us as perfect through his righteousness and because he died for our sins and they are forgiven already as if they never were.

We need to gain that position through faith. When we are saved, his Holy Spirit is in us, and becomes our comforter and our guide to keep us on the right path, following Christ. Then we can know that the human spirit may be weak, but his strength and righteousness can be in us through his Holy Spirit.

Ro. 8;1-2 KJV) There is therefore no condemnation to them which are in Christ Jesus, who walk not after the flesh, bur after the spirit. For the law of the spirit of life in Christ Jesus hath made me free from the law of sin and death.

Col. 2:9-10 (KJV) For in him dwelleth the fullness of the godhead bodily and ye are complete in him; which is the head of all principality and power.

This relationship cannot be earned or inherited. Grace is unmerited favor, because salvation in Jesus means sins are gone and a new life in Christ has been born. This is the meaning of being born again.

The books of Acts, First Corinthians, Galatians, Ephesians and Hebrews also have a lot to say about grace; a subject worthy of study. Psalms also has many good references. God's righteousness and grace lead us to a place where we are able to know our creator and Lord in such a way that we can ask and receive spiritual wisdom., By faith we surrender to the will of God who has a plan for every life. For therein the righteousness of God revealed from faith to faith as it is written, the just shall live by faith.

All the blessings God hath bestowed upon man are of his mere grace, bounty, or favor; his free undeserved favor; favor altogether undeserved; man, having no claim to the least of his mercies. It was free grace that formed man out of the dust of the ground, and breathed into him a living soul, and stamped on that soul the image of God, and put all things under his feet. The same free grace continues to us, at this day, life, and breath, and all things. For there is nothing we are, or have, or do, which can deserve the least thing at God's hand. All our works, thou, O God, hast wrought in us! These therefore are so many more instances of his free mercy, and whatever righteousness may be found in man, this also the gift of God. John Wesley

CHAPTER 10

Insight

We have already read about King Solomon asking God for wisdom to guide his people, but at the same time he was given "great insight." Worldly wisdom calls it understanding, but spiritual wisdom brings us to a depth of understanding that goes far beyond what the ungodly could ever hope to understand. It means understanding parables and prophecy and visions and is an illumination that lights the mind to the miraculous and revelations. It is inspiration from the Holy Spirit.

Seeing and perceiving are what the world calls insight. It's like getting the mind focused on something and really getting a total understanding of what is really going on. It's figuring out that there is more involved than what the eye can see. A man may seem strange because he has no social life. You might call him a workaholic until you find out he is raising six siblings all by himself. You may think your neighbor doesn't like you because he avoids speaking to you until you find out he doesn't have any good teeth and can't afford to have them removed and only needs to save himself embarrassment. A child may have a tantrum when there seems to be no reason. Later you learn he is ignored at home and just wants attention.

We need to be sure that we do not jump to conclusions when we observe the world around us and situations impress us in one way when it's not that way at all. Insight is knowing that we really know what we think we know. On the news, we see pictures of hardened criminals that look like nice people and nice people who look suspicious. Sometimes we don't know who to trust anymore. Domestic abuse goes on in what we perceive as happy families. Nice people become addicts and steal from us. Insight is very important in the world we live in.

In the Bible, insight comes to man through the Holy Spirit for all to benefit by miracles and prophecy, illumination, comprehension and revelation. Where there is spiritual wisdom, there is insight.

1 Kings 4:26 God gave Solomon wisdom and great insight.

Chr. 27:32 Jonathan, David's uncle, was a counselor, a man of insight and a scribe.

Job 34:35 says that if someone without knowledge speaks, his words lack insight.

In Proverbs, Wisdom, understanding and insight are used together many times.

In Daniel, Insight goes with wisdom and intelligence.

2 Tim. 2:7 For the lord will give you, insight into all of this.

CHAPTER 11

Conclusion

Wisdom is the ultimate success of the mind. It is the result of all the things that go on inside our brain: heart, soul, conscience, thought, knowledge, learning, feelings, emotions, perception, fear, faith, joy, sorrow, mental suffering, understanding, morality, character, insight, prudence, stupidity, sanity, courage, planning, sin, righteousness, foolishness, believing, doubting, anxiety, despair, hope, hopelessness, strength, weakness, love, hate, desperation and even more.

Worldly wisdom is not enough to give peace, love, and contentment. The Holy Spirit, the spirit of truth clears the mind of garbage and replaces it with spiritual wisdom which keeps the garbage out. True wisdom is the spirit of truth which reigns in the righteous.

Worldly wisdom begins with common sense; knowing the difference between right and wrong and choosing the right. It makes good choices and keeps us out of trouble. It seeks the good and avoids evil. It seeks knowledge and learns to function properly among others and to make a life.

Wisdom in the deepest sense is a divine gift.

Acts 6:8-10 (KJV) And Stephen full of faith and power, did great wonders and miracles among the people. Then there arose certain of the synagogue, which is called the synagogue of the Libertines and the Cyrenians, and Alexandrians and of them of Cilicia and of Asia disputing with Stephen.

He was a righteous man with wisdom obeying God against God's enemies.

1 Cor. 2:6-7 (KJV) Howbeit we speak wisdom among them that are perfect; yet not the wisdom of this world, nor the princes of this world, that come to nought. But we speak the wisdom of God in a mystery, even the hidden wisdom which God ordained before the world unto our glory.

12:8 (KJV) For to one there is given by the spirit the word of wisdom; to another the word of knowledge by means of the same spirit.

Eph. 1:17 (KJV) That the God of our Lord Jesus Christ, the father of glory, may give unto you the spirit of wisdom and revelation in the knowledge of him.

Col. 1:9 (KJV) For this cause we also, since the day we heard it, we have not ceased to pray for you and to desire that you might be filled with the knowledge of his will, in all wisdom and spiritual understanding.

3:16 (KJV)Let the word of Christ dwell in you richly in all wisdom teaching and admonishing one another in Psalms and hymns and spiritual songs singing with grace in your hearts to the Lord.

Jas. 1:5 (KJV) If any of you lack wisdom, let him ask of God that giveth to all men liberally and upbraideth not; and it shall be given him.

3:13-18 (KJV) Who is a wise man and endued with knowledge among you? Let him show it out of a good conversation his works with meekness of wisdom. But If you have bitter envying and strife in your hearts, glory not and lie not against the truth. This wisdom descendeth not from above, but is earthly, sensual, devilish. For where envying and strife is, there is confusion and every evil work. But the wisdom that is from above is first pure, then peaceable, gentle, easy to be entreated, full of mercy and good fruits, without partiality and without hypocrisy. And the fruit of righteousness is sown in peace of them that make peace.

Wisdom is the ultimate success of the mind. It is the result of all the things that go on in our brain: heart, soul, conscience, thought, knowledge, learning, feeling, emotions, perception, fear, faith, joy, sorrow, mental suffering, understanding, morality, character, insight, prudence, stupidity, sanity, courage, righteousness, planning, sin, foolishness, believing, doubting, anxiety, despair, hope, hopelessness, strength, weakness, love, hate and desperation.

Worldly wisdom is not enough to give peace, love and contentment. The Holy Spirit, the spirit of truth clears the mind of garbage and replaces it with spiritual wisdom which keeps the garbage out. True wisdom is the spirit of truth that dwells in the righteous.

Worldly wisdom develops by necessity; it's called survival. Spiritual wisdom comes from God and brings revival.

Bibliography

NIV Study Bible 1984 Zondervan

New Unger's Bible Dictionary 1988 Moody Press

Strongest NIV Exhaustive concordance 1999 Zondervan

Webster's New Explorer Dictionary 2000 Federal Street Press

Handbook of Theological Terms 1964 Van A. Harvey Collier Books

King James Bible, International Bible Society

Wesleyana, Ten Talents Publishing LLC

Coming Soon

Book 4 'Fear, Faith, and Fire' Spring 2017

Lost, searching, found.

Take a journey from the chaos of this world to the wisdom and confidence of a faith that brings the power of Holy Spirit fire into a victorious Christian life.

Meet the author daily at her blog on Face Book.

Printed in the United States
By Bookmasters